UNDERSTANDING RELIGIONS

Pilgrimages and Journeys

Katherine Prior

Wayland

Understanding Religions

Birth Customs
Death Customs
Food and Fasting
Initiation Customs
Marriage Customs
Pilgrimages and Journeys

About this book

This book looks at the very old custom of pilgrimage as it is practised in six of the world's major religions. Pilgrimage is an important part of religious life because it is a form of worship that everybody can take part in, regardless of their wealth or education.

Each chapter compares the approaches of different religions to one aspect of religious journeying. The book looks at why people go on pilgrimages, where they go, how they behave and dress on the journey and what they do at their destination. It also describes some pilgrimages and pilgrims from the past and explains some of the interaction between different religions.

The children's quotations in **Pilgrimages and Journeys** will encourage young readers to imagine what it would be like to be a pilgrim themselves.

Editor: Joanna Housley
Designer: Malcolm Walker

First published in 1992 by
Wayland (Publishers) Limited
61 Western Road, Hove
East Sussex, BN3 1JD, England

© Copyright 1992 Wayland (Publishers) Limited

British Library Cataloguing in Publication Data
Prior, Katherine
   Pilgrimages and Journeys. (Understanding Religions Series)
   I. Title II. Series
   291.4

ISBN 0 7502 0422 2

Typeset by Kudos Editorial and Design Services
Printed in Italy by G Canale C.S.p.A. Turin

Contents

Words that appear in **bold** in the text are
explained in the glossary on page 30.

Introduction

A pilgrimage is a religious journey and the people who go on pilgrimages are called pilgrims. They are not like business travellers or tourists on holiday. They travel to places that are holy in their religion because they want to get close to their God.

Pilgrimage is a very popular form of **worship**. Every year millions of pilgrims from many different religions make special religious journeys. Anyone can be a pilgrim, whether they are rich or poor, male or female, old or young.

Left Huge numbers of Muslims go on a pilgrimage to Mecca for the Hajj every year.

What is a holy site?

A holy site is a place where people can feel very close to their God and their religion. Every religion has places which are special to it. Some are very busy and in the centre of big, bustling cities. Pilgrims can get to them in aeroplanes, trains and cars. But some holy sites are high up in snow-covered mountains and pilgrims have to climb up the slippery slopes on foot or riding on the backs of donkeys.

Below The Hindu God, Rama, was born in Ayodhya in north India. This is one of many temples there dedicated to Rama.

In India, Hindus have many holy sites which are linked to stories of how their gods and goddesses came down from heaven to live on earth. Wherever a god was born or lived became a holy place, and today Hindus go on pilgrimages to these places because they hope to see the spot where a god travelled between heaven and earth. Hindus who worship the god Rama go on pilgrimages to his birthplace in Ayodhya in north India. Hindus who worship the god Krishna make pilgrimages to the towns of Brindavan and Mathura where Krishna was born and grew up.

Buddhists have holy sites in India too. They show where important things happened in the life of the Buddha. The Buddha was a prince who lived in India about 2,500 years ago. Buddhists do not worship him as a god, but they know that he lived a very holy life and learnt the secret of living in perfect peace.

At Buddh Gaya pilgrims can see the holy tree where the Buddha sat and prayed for a long time and learnt how to live without selfishness or greed. This is called the Tree of Enlightenment. At Sarnath they can see where the Buddha began to teach his **disciples** the first lessons of Buddhism. Pilgrims still go to these holy sites today to try to learn and understand more about the Buddha's teaching.

Varanasi is a holy site for Hindus because it is on the bank of the holy river Ganges. Radhika was ten years old when she visited Varanasi with her parents:

'Early on our first morning we climbed down the steps to take a bath in the Ganges. It was still almost dark and the water was very cold! A priest helped us say our prayers and I lit a small floating candle as an offering to the Goddess of the Ganges.'

Right An important holy site for Buddhists is this tree in Buddh Gaya, India. It is known as the Tree of Enlightenment, and Buddhists believe this is where the Buddha learnt how to live without any desires or suffering.

The whole of Israel is special for Jews. Thousands of years ago their God promised them that they would always be able to feel his presence in Jerusalem. To give thanks to God for his promise, King Solomon ordered a magnificent temple of stone to be built in the city. Jewish men made three pilgrimages a year to the temple until it was destroyed

by the Romans in CE 70. Today only a single wall is left. This is called the Western Wall and Jews come from all over the world to pray there and feel close to God.

Above The Western Wall in Jerusalem is all that remains of the Jewish temple first built there by King Solomon nearly 3,000 years ago.

Christians regard all of the land of Israel where Jesus Christ lived and taught as the Holy Land, but the most important holy sites are in Jerusalem where Jesus died and came back to life. Jesus was born almost 1,000 years after Solomon had built the Temple of the

Jews. Christians believe that he was the son of God and that God sent him to earth to show people how to worship the one God and obtain **eternal** life. But Jesus' teaching upset the Jewish leaders and Roman rulers of Jerusalem and he was put to death at the time of year now called Easter. Every Easter pilgrims gather at the hill of Calvary where he was **crucified** and thank God for sending his son to teach them about Christianity.

Muslims go on pilgrimages to places that were important in the life of the

Below The great courtyard of the Sacred Mosque at Mecca can hold up to 500,000 pilgrims. At prayer times everyone kneels on prayer mats facing the Kaaba in the centre.

Prophet Muhammad. Muhammad was born almost 1,500 years ago. Muslims believe that he was the holy messenger of Allah, who was sent to earth to teach people to worship only one God. Allah is the Muslim name for God.

The city of Mecca in Saudi Arabia is the most important holy site for Muslims. Here, in an ancient building called the Kaaba, or God's House, Muhammad stopped his countrymen from praying to **idols** or statues of different gods and he showed them how to worship the one God, Allah. Every year millions of

Above The beautiful Golden Temple in Amritsar, India, is the holiest centre for Sikhs.

Muslims come to Mecca to worship Allah.

Sikhs have many holy sites associated with the lives of their ten **Gurus**, or holy teachers. The most sacred is the Golden Temple in the city of Amritsar in India. The temple is like a golden island floating in the middle of a large lake. The tenth Guru was Gobind Singh and he instructed all his followers that they should come and bathe in the holy waters that surround the Golden Temple.

Martyrs

Every religion has good teachers and leaders. Sometimes these holy men and women let themselves be killed by their enemies rather than give up their religious beliefs. People who do this are called martyrs. They show that they love their God more than they love their own life. When a holy person is martyred people will often go on a pilgrimage to the place where he or she is buried.

One of the most famous Sikh martyrs was the ninth Guru, Tegh Bahadur. 300 years ago he was beheaded on the orders of the Mogul Emperor. A Sikh temple, the Gurdwara Rakab Ganj, was built at the place in Delhi, India, where Tegh Bahadur's body was **cremated** and every year thousands of Sikhs make pilgrimages there to honour the sacrifice that he made for his religion.

Below Sikhs gather at the Gurdwara Rakab Ganj to remember the life of the ninth Guru, Tegh Bahadur.

Pilgrimages in the past

Most religions are very old and many have grown and changed a lot since their beginnings. Some religions have spread a long way from the countries where they started. New holy sites appeared wherever the religion went, at places where a holy person died or was buried, or where a miracle happened.

Buddhism spread from India to Sri Lanka, Burma, Thailand, Nepal, Tibet,

Above The Temple of the Tooth in Sri Lanka contains a tooth that is said to have been one of the Buddha's. Many pilgrims visit places that are believed to contain **relics** from religious leaders.

China and Japan. All of these countries have holy sites connected with the teachers who first brought Buddhism to them. There are also holy sites which pilgrims visit where relics or remains of the Buddha are kept safely. In the town of Kandy in Sri Lanka there is a famous temple which preserves a tooth said to have been one of the Buddha's.

After Jesus Christ's death, Christianity spread to Europe, then to the Americas. In 1531, at Guadalupe in Mexico, a poor man had a **vision** of the Virgin Mary, the mother of Jesus Christ. She told him to

Below Roman Catholics worship at a shrine to the Virgin Mary in Guadalupe, Mexico. A special service is held there every year to celebrate the appearance of the Virgin Mary to a local man.

build a **shrine** in her name at Guadalupe and, ever since then, thousands of Roman Catholics from all parts of Latin America have travelled there each year on 12 December to celebrate Our Lady of Guadalupe Day.

Islam spread very widely from its beginnings in Arabia. In Asia and Africa many Muslims go on pilgrimages to the tombs of the holy teachers who brought Islam to their country.

Battles over holy sites

All religions teach people to be good and kind, but often members of different religions fight one another because they want to prove that their religion is the right one and that their idea of God is the best one. Some people will go to war if their holy sites are being controlled by members of a different religion.

Judaism, Christianity and Islam all began in the countries bordering the Red Sea, in the area that we now call the Middle East. The three religions have many holy sites that are very close together and Jews, Christians and Muslims have fought a lot of battles over them.

The biggest battles of all were The Crusades in the **Middle Ages**. Thousands of Christians marched from Europe to the land where Jesus had lived to fight Muslims who were living there.

Above In Jerusalem Muslims and Jews worship very near to each other. Here you can see that the Muslim Dome of the Rock overlooks the Jewish Western Wall.

Nowadays Jerusalem is controlled by the Jewish state of Israel, but there are still problems with its holy sites. Hundreds of years ago the Muslims built a beautiful **mausoleum** on the site of the old Temple of the Jews. It is called the Dome of the Rock, and it marks the place where Muhammad rode up to heaven on his sacred horse. For Muslims it is a very holy site, but it is also a holy site for Jews because the Western Wall is nearby.

In India there are holy sites that are claimed by both Hindus and Muslims. Muslim invaders sometimes destroyed Hindu temples and built mosques on their ruins.

Why do people go on pilgrimages today?

People go on pilgrimages for many different reasons, but all pilgrims hope that they will feel closer to their God by visiting a holy site.

Giving thanks and asking favours

Sometimes people go on pilgrimages when something special has happened to them. A sick person who gets better, or a woman who has had a baby may go on a pilgrimage to give thanks for their good fortune.

Some people go on pilgrimages to ask their God for a favour, and promise to make another pilgrimage if their prayers are answered. Perhaps they want a new business to be successful, or their children to pass their exams at school, or rain to fall and make their crops grow.

Praying for good health

Every religion has holy sites where pilgrims who are sick pray to be made healthy. They have illnesses which their doctor cannot cure, so they ask their God to make them better.

At Lourdes in France there is a spring of water which is believed to have

Above The temples at Hindu holy sites often have beautiful carvings like these.

Above Roman Catholics visit Lourdes in France because they believe the water there is holy. Sick pilgrims bathe in the water in the hope of being cured.

healing powers. It was discovered only one hundred and fifty years ago, when the Virgin Mary appeared in a vision to a peasant girl and showed her where the spring was. Nowadays Roman Catholics who are ill go to Lourdes from all over Europe to bathe in the spring water and to pray to the Virgin Mary to be cured.

In India there is a very old tree growing by the sacred tank of the Sikh Golden Temple. Four hundred years ago a **leper** took a bath in the pond near the tree and was miraculously cured of his disease. Since then many Sikhs have bathed at that spot hoping to be cured of their illnesses.

Even healthy pilgrims often have baths at holy sites. This is because many religions use water as a **symbol** or sign of purity. When pilgrims take a bath it is a way of showing that they are washing their hearts and minds clean of any bad thoughts.

Above   Sikhs believe that this tree growing beside the Golden Temple in Amritsar has special healing powers. Sikhs who are ill hope to be cured by bathing in the water around it.

Coming together

In Islam pilgrimage is compulsory. Every adult Muslim who can afford it and who is healthy must go on a pilgrimage to Mecca at least once in his or her lifetime. This pilgrimage is called the Hajj and it only happens for a few days each year in Dhu al-Hijjah, the twelfth month of the

Ali was twelve when he and his father travelled from Indonesia for the Hajj:
'It was wonderful, but a bit frightening, to see all those thousands and thousands of people from so many different places. We had a guide who explained things for us because we couldn't understand the language. But even though people looked different and spoke other languages we were still all Muslims and we all said the same prayers and did the same things. I was really proud to be a Muslim when I saw everyone praying together.'

Islamic calendar. The Hajj brings millions of Muslims together from all around the world and shows them that they belong to one enormous family.

In Judaism pilgrimage brings people together too. There is no special time for making a pilgrimage to the Western Wall in Jerusalem, but even if a Jew visits the Wall alone she or he will still get a very precious feeling of belonging to a large religious family. The Western Wall has a lot of Jewish history in it, and making a pilgrimage there is like having a magical meeting with all the Jews of the past.

Below Ritual bathing is an important part of many religions. Hindus bathe in the River Ganges because they believe its water is holy.

The journey

The journey to the holy site is a very important part of a pilgrimage. Before modern transport it could be very hard to get to a holy site, but most pilgrims did not complain about their difficulties because they were happy to suffer for their religion.

Nowadays some pilgrims travel in such comfort that they look like ordinary tourists. Jews, Christians and Muslims can fly to the Middle East from almost anywhere in the world. Hindus, Sikhs and Buddhists can join pilgrimage bus-tours in India which take them to several of their holy sites in just a few days. Christians can catch special pilgrimage trains to Lourdes in France; prayers and hymns are broadcast throughout the train and there are special ambulance carriages for the sick pilgrims. Many governments and religious organizations spend a lot of money making the journey comfortable for pilgrims.

Even today, however, some pilgrims do not take the easy way to get to their holy site. They are prepared to give up a lot of their time and all the comforts of modern travel to show how much they love their God. Some Christian pilgrims still walk across northern Spain to the

Below Pilgrims sometimes suffer for their religion. By walking barefoot in snow to a holy site, this pilgrim is showing that he can put up with pain for his God.

Right Inside the cathedral at Santiago de Compostela in Spain Christian pilgrims hug a statue of St James. He was an early Christian martyr.

tomb of St James, an early Christian martyr, at Santiago de Compostela. This is called the Way of St James. Some Hindu pilgrims walk barefoot all the way to their holy sites to show that they are prepared to put up with pain for their God. Occasionally some Buddhist and Hindu pilgrims will even cover long distances crawling on their hands and knees. The pilgrims' desire to serve their religion is shown by their willingness to suffer for it.

Dressing and behaving like a pilgrim

Pilgrims should prepare themselves properly for their journey and show that they are really thinking about their religious duties while they are travelling. They often wear special clothes so that along the way other people will recognize them as pilgrims and treat them with kindness and respect.

Hindus have a holy bath at home and say special prayers with their family priest before they start on a pilgrimage. For the whole journey they have to keep their thoughts clean and not get angry or shout at any person or animal. Often their clothes are white or saffron (deep yellow). These are the colours that Hindus wear when they want to show that they are not interested in the everyday things going on around them and that they are only thinking about their God.

A lot of Buddhist pilgrims, especially monks, wear saffron-coloured robes too. Buddhist pilgrims must remember to treat the Buddha and other holy teachers with respect. They should not laugh or be too light-hearted when they are visiting holy sites.

Below Buddhist monks in Thailand are easy to recognize in their orange robes.

Above A Muslim family prepare themselves for the Hajj. They are all dressed in the special clothes for pilgrims called *ihram*.

Among Christians, Roman Catholics confess their **sins** to their priest before they set out on a pilgrimage. This helps them to travel with only goodness in their hearts. Many Christian pilgrims do not look very different from ordinary travellers, although they often wear a badge to show where they are going. Pilgrims going to Santiago de Compostela wear a cockle shell which shows that their holy site is by the sea. Pilgrims in the Middle Ages used the shell as a spoon or food scoop.

Muslims going on the Hajj have a special type of dress called *ihram*, which they put on before they reach Mecca. For men this is two pieces of plain white cotton cloth. One is folded around the waist and the other hangs over the left shoulder. Muslim women wear a long white cotton dress. Before they put on *ihram* the pilgrims must have a **purifying** bath and announce their intention of performing the Hajj.

As long as they are wearing *ihram* the pilgrims must not tell lies or get angry. They must not wear perfume, make-up or jewellery. They must not look at themselves in mirrors. If they did any of these things it would show that they were more concerned about themselves than about Allah. The pilgrims must show that they are thinking about Allah all the time.

Worshipping at the holy site

Pilgrims often have special things to do at their holy site to make sure that their pilgrimage is a successful one and that their God has heard their prayers.

For Jews a pilgrimage to the Western Wall is a solemn occasion, because the Wall reminds them of the destruction of the Temple. On a special date, 9 Ab in the Jewish calendar, which is the anniversary of the Temple's destruction, many pilgrims gather at the Wall to mourn their loss. The pilgrims used to cry so loudly on this sad anniversary that non-

Rachel, an American girl who went to the Western Wall, said:
'Some of my friends at home think it is funny that we keep the men and the women apart, but we have to concentrate on praying. We shouldn't be trying to see what the boys on the other side of the fence look like.'

Left Jewish pilgrims at the Western Wall sometimes write their prayers on pieces of paper, and push them between the stones.

Above Jerusalem is also important to Christians. On Good Friday, the day Jesus died, Christians walk through the streets of the city. Jesus was forced to walk through Jerusalem carrying the cross on which he would later die.

Jewish people nicknamed it the 'Wailing Wall'. Men and women are separated by a fence at the Wall. The men pray on the left and the women pray on the right.

In Jerusalem in Easter Week Roman Catholic and **Orthodox Christians** follow the last movements that Jesus Christ made in the days before he was nailed to the cross and died on Good Friday. On these days the pilgrims are sorrowful. They do not wear bright clothes and many of them **fast** or eat only a little food. On Easter Sunday, which is the day they believe Jesus came back to life, the pilgrims are joyful and sing hymns praising God for his power and goodness. They eat rich food and put on their best clothes.

The Hajj is a complicated pilgrimage and many Muslims hire guides who tell them what to do on each day of their visit to Mecca. An important part of the Hajj is called the 'standing'. Pilgrims stand all day on the Mount of Mercy at Arafat to remember that this is where Muhammad gave his farewell sermon on his own pilgrimage. Near the end of the Hajj the pilgrims kill a goat or sheep in **sacrifice**. This shows that they are willing to give something up to Allah

Below A traditional form of Hindu worship is *puja*, when an offering is made before a sacred fire. This family is burning candles in front of the image of a Hindu God.

Above These Buddhist women in Tibet are lying face down before an image of the Buddha. This shows that they are humble in worship.

and reminds them to be **charitable**. They must give a portion of the meat to the poor.

When Hindu pilgrims reach their holy sites they take a holy bath in a river or tank and pray for their sins to be washed away. Often a priest says the prayers for them. After bathing the pilgrims have their heads shaved, although most women just have one or two locks of their hair cut off. At really large Hindu festivals the government has trouble getting rid of the mountains of hair!

When their bodies and hearts are properly cleaned the pilgrims are ready to face their God in a temple. They will pray before him or her and give little gifts of money, flowers and candles. Some holy sites have many temples with many gods and goddesses. A pilgrim can be busy for several days going to see all of them.

At Buddhist holy sites the pilgrims show respect to the Buddha and other great teachers by bowing or lying face-down on the ground before images of them. This is called prostration. It is a way for the pilgrims to show that they are humble and unimportant before the wisdom of their teachers.

Every Sikh holy site has a temple called a gurdwara which contains a copy of the Guru Granth Sahib, the holy book of the Sikhs. Sikhs bow down before the book as a way of showing it respect. The Sikhs were taught by the Gurus to be charitable and to treat all people as equals. At holy sites they follow these principles by opening kitchens which give free food to anyone who comes. The kitchens are called *langars*. The food is usually vegetarian (without meat) and everyone eats together, sitting on the floor. Pilgrims often do a good deed while they are at a holy site. They may help serve the food in the *langar* or perhaps sweep the floors.

Manjeet, a Sikh boy who has been to the Golden Temple, said:
'We take our shoes off before we go into a gurdwara. At the Golden Temple, I cleaned some of the other pilgrims' shoes. Some of them were really dusty and a bit smelly! But it is important that we do jobs like that. We have to remember that God likes even simple work and that no one is too important to work for God.'

The way home

Many pilgrims like to take something back to their homes to remind them of their pilgrimage. This is often some earth or water that they have collected from the holy site and which they keep safely for the rest of their lives.

A pilgrim returning home is someone special. Hindu pilgrims receive a warm welcome from their family and friends. Often they have a feast and everybody eats sweets brought back from the holy site. Bottles containing water from the Ganges may be placed in home shrines. Christian pilgrims are sometimes asked to tell the people in their local church about their experiences. Muslims who have returned from the Hajj are given the title Hajji, so that even strangers will know that they have been to Mecca.

Right Visitors to the holy spring at Lourdes may collect some of the water and take it home with them.

Glossary

CE Christian Era. A term used by non-Christians when talking about a date after the birth of Jesus.

Charitable Kind and generous to others.

Cremate To burn a dead body.

Crucify To kill someone by hanging them on a cross and leaving them without food or water.

Disciple A follower of a religious leader.

Eternal Lasting for ever.

Fast To go without food.

Gurus Hindu or Sikh religious leaders and teachers.

Idol A statue of a God.

Leper Someone who suffers from leprosy, a disease in which parts of the body lose their feeling and rot away.

Mausoleum A large, grand tomb.

Middle Ages The period in European history from 500 to 1500.

Orthodox Christians Members of a division of Christianity that is strong in Eastern Europe and Russia.

Purify To clean thoroughly.

Relics The remains of a holy person's body and his or her possessions.

Sacrifice To make an offering to, or give up something for a God.

Shrine A sacred place in which the holy relics of a saint are kept.

Sins Bad thoughts and actions.

Symbol A sign for showing something that is hard to explain in ordinary words.

Vision The magical appearance of a God or saint, as if they were being seen in a dream.

Vow A solemn promise.

Worship To show devotion and respect to God.

Further information

Books to read

The following books contain more useful information about pilgrimages and journeys throughout the world:
Growing up in Islam by Janet Ardavan (Longman, 1990)
Pilgrimages Schools Council (Hart-Davis Educational, 1977)
Pilgrimages and Crusades by Gillian Evans (Chambers, 1976)
The Pilgrim's Way by Gwilym T Jones (Welsh National Centre for Religious Education, 1987)
Pilgrimage by Jon Mayled (Wayland, 1986)
Islam by Sue Penney (Heinemann Educational, 1987)

Picture acknowledgements

The publishers wish to thank the following for supplying the photographs in this book:
J Allan Cash 8, 10, 12, 16, 19 (right), 24 (both), 25, 26; Cephas Picture Library 29 (Frank B Higham); David Cumming 21; Eye Ubiquitous 19 (left, Peter Sanders), 27 (Julia Waterlow); D Henderson 18; Hutchison Library 7 (J Pate), 13 (Liba Taylor), 17 (Bernard Régent), 20 (Dave Brinicombe), 23 (Bernard Gérard); Christine Osborne Pictures 28; Ann & Bury Peerless 5, 11; Tony Stone Worldwide 4 (Nabeel Turner), 9 (Nabeel Turner), 15 (Hugh Sitton), 22; Zefa cover.

Index

Numbers in **bold** indicate photographs